FLORIDA EVIDENC
2017 Edition

I0074950

Updated through January 1, 2017

Michigan Legal Publishing Ltd.
QUICK DESK REFERENCE SERIES™

WE WELCOME YOUR FEEDBACK: info@michlp.com

ISBN-13: 978-1-64002-007-8
ISBN-10: 1-64002-007-1

Contents

§ 90.101. Short title

This chapter shall be known and may be cited as the "Florida Evidence Code."

§ 90.102. Construction

This chapter shall replace and supersede existing statutory or common law in conflict with its provisions.

§ 90.103. Scope; applicability

(1) Unless otherwise provided by statute, this code applies to the same proceedings that the general law of evidence applied to before the effective date of this code.

(2) This act shall apply to criminal proceedings related to crimes committed after the effective date of this code and to civil actions and all other proceedings pending on or brought after October 1, 1981.

(3) Nothing in this act shall operate to repeal or modify the parol evidence rule.

§ 90.104. Rulings on evidence

(1) A court may predicate error, set aside or reverse a judgment, or grant a new trial on the basis of admitted or excluded evidence when a substantial right of the party is adversely affected and:

(a) When the ruling is one admitting evidence, a timely objection or motion to strike appears on the record, stating the specific ground of objection if the specific ground was not apparent from the context; or

(b) When the ruling is one excluding evidence, the substance of the evidence was made known to the court by offer of proof or was apparent from the context within which the questions were asked.

If the court has made a definitive ruling on the record admitting or excluding evidence, either at or before trial, a party need not renew an objection or offer of proof to preserve a claim of error for appeal.

(2) In cases tried by a jury, a court shall conduct proceedings, to the maximum extent practicable, in such a manner as to prevent inadmissible evidence from being suggested to the jury by any means.

(3) Nothing in this section shall preclude a court from taking notice of fundamental errors affecting substantial rights, even though such errors were not brought to the attention of the trial judge.

§ 90.105. Preliminary questions

(1) Except as provided in subsection (2), the court shall determine preliminary questions concerning the qualification of a person to be a witness, the existence of a privilege, or the admissibility of evidence.
(2) When the relevancy of evidence depends upon the existence of a preliminary fact, the court shall admit the proffered evidence when there is prima facie evidence sufficient to support a finding of the preliminary fact. If prima facie evidence is not introduced to support a finding of the preliminary fact, the court may admit the proffered evidence subject to the subsequent introduction of prima facie evidence of the preliminary fact.
(3) Hearings on the admissibility of confessions shall be conducted out of the hearing of the jury. Hearings on other preliminary matters shall be similarly conducted when the interests of justice require or when an accused is a witness, if he or she so requests.

§ 90.106. Summing up and comment by judge

A judge may not sum up the evidence or comment to the jury upon the weight of the evidence, the credibility of the witnesses, or the guilt of the accused.

§ 90.107. Limited admissibility

When evidence that is admissible as to one party or for one purpose, but inadmissible as to another party or for another purpose, is admitted, the court, upon request, shall restrict such evidence to its proper scope and so inform the jury at the time it is admitted.

§ 90.108. Introduction of related writings or recorded statements

(1) When a writing or recorded statement or part thereof is introduced by a party, an adverse party may require him or her at that time to introduce any other part or any other writing or recorded statement that in fairness ought to be considered contemporaneously. An adverse party is not bound by evidence introduced under this section.

(2) The report of a court reporter, when certified to by the court reporter as being a correct transcript of the testimony and proceedings in the case, is prima facie a correct statement of such testimony and proceedings.

§ 90.201. Matters which must be judicially noticed

A court shall take judicial notice of:
(1) Decisional, constitutional, and public statutory law and resolutions of the Florida Legislature and the Congress of the United States.
(2) Florida rules of court that have statewide application, its own rules, and the rules of United States courts adopted by the United States Supreme Court.
(3) Rules of court of the United States Supreme Court and of the United States Courts of Appeal.

§ 90.202. Matters which may be judicially noticed

A court may take judicial notice of the following matters, to the extent that they are not embraced within s. 90.201:
(1) Special, local, and private acts and resolutions of the Congress of the United States and of the Florida Legislature.
(2) Decisional, constitutional, and public statutory law of every other state, territory, and jurisdiction of the United States.
(3) Contents of the Federal Register.
(4) Laws of foreign nations and of an organization of nations.
(5) Official actions of the legislative, executive, and judicial departments of the United States and of any state, territory, or jurisdiction of the United States.
(6) Records of any court of this state or of any court of record of the United States or of any state, territory, or jurisdiction of the United States.
(7) Rules of court of any court of this state or of any court of record of the United States or of any other state, territory, or jurisdiction of the United States.
(8) Provisions of all municipal and county charters and charter amendments of this state, provided they are available in printed copies or as certified copies.
(9) Rules promulgated by governmental agencies of this state which are published in the Florida Administrative Code or in bound written copies.

(10) Duly enacted ordinances and resolutions of municipalities and counties located in Florida, provided such ordinances and resolutions are available in printed copies or as certified copies.

(11) Facts that are not subject to dispute because they are generally known within the territorial jurisdiction of the court.

(12) Facts that are not subject to dispute because they are capable of accurate and ready determination by resort to sources whose accuracy cannot be questioned.

(13) Official seals of governmental agencies and departments of the United States and of any state, territory, or jurisdiction of the United States.

§ 90.203. Compulsory judicial notice upon request

A court shall take judicial notice of any matter in s. 90.202 when a party requests it and:

(1) Gives each adverse party timely written notice of the request, proof of which is filed with the court, to enable the adverse party to prepare to meet the request.

(2) Furnishes the court with sufficient information to enable it to take judicial notice of the matter.

§ 90.204. Determination of propriety of judicial notice and nature of matter noticed

(1) When a court determines upon its own motion that judicial notice of a matter should be taken or when a party requests such notice and shows good cause for not complying with s. 90.203(1), the court shall afford each party reasonable opportunity to present information relevant to the propriety of taking judicial notice and to the nature of the matter noticed.

(2) In determining the propriety of taking judicial notice of a matter or the nature thereof, a court may use any source of pertinent and reliable information, whether or not furnished by a party, without regard to any exclusionary rule except a valid claim of privilege and except for the exclusions provided in s. 90.403.

(3) If a court resorts to any documentary source of information not received in open court, the court shall make the information and its source a part of the record in the action and shall afford each party reasonable opportunity to challenge such information, and to offer additional information, before judicial notice of the matter is taken.

(4) In family cases, the court may take judicial notice of any matter described in s. 90.202(6) when imminent danger to persons or property has been alleged and it is impractical to give prior notice to the parties of the intent to take judicial notice. Opportunity to present evidence relevant to the propriety of taking judicial notice under subsection (1) may be deferred until after judicial action has been taken. If judicial notice is taken under this subsection, the court shall, within 2 business days, file a notice in the pending case of the matters judicially noticed. For purposes of this subsection, the term "family cases" has the same meaning as provided in the Rules of Judicial Administration.

§ 90.205. Denial of a request for judicial notice

Upon request of counsel, when a court denies a request to take judicial notice of any matter, the court shall inform the parties at the earliest practicable time and shall indicate for the record that it has denied the request.

§ 90.206. Instructing jury on judicial notice

The court may instruct the jury during the trial to accept as a fact a matter judicially noticed.

§ 90.207. Judicial notice by trial court in subsequent proceedings

The failure or refusal of a court to take judicial notice of a matter does not preclude a court from taking judicial notice of the matter in subsequent proceedings, in accordance with the procedure specified in ss. 90.201-90.206.

§ 90.301. Presumption defined; inferences

(1) For the purposes of this chapter, a presumption is an assumption of fact which the law makes from the existence of another fact or group of facts found or otherwise established.
(2) Except for presumptions that are conclusive under the law from which they arise, a presumption is rebuttable.
(3) Nothing in this chapter shall prevent the drawing of an inference that is appropriate.
(4) Sections 90.301-90.304 are applicable only in civil actions or proceedings.

§ 90.302. Classification of rebuttable presumptions

Every rebuttable presumption is either:

(1) A presumption affecting the burden of producing evidence and requiring the trier of fact to assume the existence of the presumed fact, unless credible evidence sufficient to sustain a finding of the nonexistence of the presumed fact is introduced, in which event, the existence or nonexistence of the presumed fact shall be determined from the evidence without regard to the presumption; or

(2) A presumption affecting the burden of proof that imposes upon the party against whom it operates the burden of proof concerning the nonexistence of the presumed fact.

§ 90.303. Presumption affecting the burden of producing evidence defined

In a civil action or proceeding, unless otherwise provided by statute, a presumption established primarily to facilitate the determination of the particular action in which the presumption is applied, rather than to implement public policy, is a presumption affecting the burden of producing evidence.

§ 90.304. Presumption affecting the burden of proof defined

In civil actions, all rebuttable presumptions which are not defined in s. 90.303 are presumptions affecting the burden of proof.

§ 90.401. Definition of relevant evidence

Relevant evidence is evidence tending to prove or disprove a material fact.

§ 90.402. Admissibility of relevant evidence

All relevant evidence is admissible, except as provided by law.

§ 90.4025. Admissibility of paternity determination in certain criminal prosecutions

If a person less than 18 years of age gives birth to a child and the paternity of that child is established under chapter 742, such evidence of paternity is admissible in a criminal prosecution under ss. 794.011, 794.05, 800.04, and 827.04(3).

§ 90.4026. Statements expressing sympathy; admissibility; definitions

(1) As used in this section:
 (a) "Accident" means an occurrence resulting in injury or death to one or more persons which is not the result of willful action by a party.
 (b) "Benevolent gestures" means actions that convey a sense of compassion or commiseration emanating from human impulses.
 (c) "Family" means the spouse, parent, grandparent, stepmother, stepfather, child, grandchild, brother, sister, half-brother, half-sister, adopted child of parent, or spouse's parent of an injured party.
(2) The portion of statements, writings, or benevolent gestures expressing sympathy or a general sense of benevolence relating to the pain, suffering, or death of a person involved in an accident and made to that person or to the family of that person shall be inadmissible as evidence in a civil action. A statement of fault, however, which is part of, or in addition to, any of the above shall be admissible pursuant to this section.

§ 90.403. Exclusion on grounds of prejudice or confusion

Relevant evidence is inadmissible if its probative value is substantially outweighed by the danger of unfair prejudice, confusion of issues, misleading the jury, or needless presentation of cumulative evidence. This section shall not be construed to mean that evidence of the existence of available third-party benefits is inadmissible.

§ 90.404. Character evidence; when admissible

(1) **Character Evidence Generally**. Evidence of a person's character or a trait of character is inadmissible to prove action in conformity with it on a particular occasion, except:
 (a) *Character of accused*. Evidence of a pertinent trait of character offered by an accused, or by the prosecution to rebut the trait.
 (b) *Character of victim*.
   1. Except as provided in s. 794.022, evidence of a pertinent trait of character of the victim of the crime offered by an accused, or by the prosecution to rebut the trait; or

      2.   Evidence of a character trait of peacefulness of the victim offered by the prosecution in a homicide case to rebut evidence that the victim was the aggressor.

(c) *Character of witness.* Evidence of the character of a witness, as provided in ss. 90.608-90.610.

(2) **Other Crimes, Wrongs, or Acts**.

(a) Similar fact evidence of other crimes, wrongs, or acts is admissible when relevant to prove a material fact in issue, including, but not limited to, proof of motive, opportunity, intent, preparation, plan, knowledge, identity, or absence of mistake or accident, but it is inadmissible when the evidence is relevant solely to prove bad character or propensity.

(b)

      1.   In a criminal case in which the defendant is charged with a crime involving child molestation, evidence of the defendant's commission of other crimes, wrongs, or acts of child molestation is admissible and may be considered for its bearing on any matter to which it is relevant.

      2.   For the purposes of this paragraph, the term "child molestation" means conduct proscribed by s. 787.025(2)(c), s. 787.06(3)(g), former s. 787.06(3)(h), s. 794.011, excluding s. 794.011(10), s. 794.05, former s. 796.03, former s. 796.035, s. 800.04, s. 827.071, s. 847.0135(5), s. 847.0145, or s. 985.701(1) when committed against a person 16 years of age or younger.

(c)

      1.   In a criminal case in which the defendant is charged with a sexual offense, evidence of the defendant's commission of other crimes, wrongs, or acts involving a sexual offense is admissible and may be considered for its bearing on any matter to which it is relevant.

      2.   For the purposes of this paragraph, the term "sexual offense" means conduct proscribed by s. 787.025(2)(c), s. 787.06(3)(b), (d), (f), or (g), former s. 787.06(3)(h), s. 794.011, excluding s. 794.011(10), s. 794.05, former s. 796.03, former s. 796.035, s. 825.1025(2)(b), s. 827.071, s. 847.0135(5), s. 847.0145, or s. 985.701(1).

(d)

      1.   When the state in a criminal action intends to offer evidence of other criminal offenses under paragraph (a), paragraph (b),

or paragraph (c), no fewer than 10 days before trial, the state shall furnish to the defendant or to the defendant's counsel a written statement of the acts or offenses it intends to offer, describing them with the particularity required of an indictment or information. No notice is required for evidence of offenses used for impeachment or on rebuttal.

2. When the evidence is admitted, the court shall, if requested, charge the jury on the limited purpose for which the evidence is received and is to be considered. After the close of the evidence, the jury shall be instructed on the limited purpose for which the evidence was received and that the defendant cannot be convicted for a charge not included in the indictment or information.

(3) Nothing in this section affects the admissibility of evidence under s. 90.610.

§ 90.405. Methods of proving character

(1) **Reputation**. When evidence of the character of a person or of a trait of that person's character is admissible, proof may be made by testimony about that person's reputation.

(2) **Specific Instances of Conduct**. When character or a trait of character of a person is an essential element of a charge, claim, or defense, proof may be made of specific instances of that person's conduct.

§ 90.406. Routine practice

Evidence of the routine practice of an organization, whether corroborated or not and regardless of the presence of eyewitnesses, is admissible to prove that the conduct of the organization on a particular occasion was in conformity with the routine practice.

§ 90.407. Subsequent remedial measures

Evidence of measures taken after an injury or harm caused by an event, which measures if taken before the event would have made injury or harm less likely to occur, is not admissible to prove negligence, the existence of a product defect, or culpable conduct in connection with the event. This rule does not require the exclusion of evidence of subsequent remedial measures when offered for another purpose, such as proving ownership, control, or the feasibility of precautionary measures, if controverted, or impeachment.

§ 90.408. Compromise and offers to compromise

Evidence of an offer to compromise a claim which was disputed as to validity or amount, as well as any relevant conduct or statements made in negotiations concerning a compromise, is inadmissible to prove liability or absence of liability for the claim or its value.

§ 90.409. Payment of medical and similar expenses

Evidence of furnishing, or offering or promising to pay, medical or hospital expenses or other damages occasioned by an injury or accident is inadmissible to prove liability for the injury or accident.

§ 90.410. Offer to plead guilty; nolo contendere; withdrawn pleas of guilty

Evidence of a plea of guilty, later withdrawn; a plea of nolo contendere; or an offer to plead guilty or nolo contendere to the crime charged or any other crime is inadmissible in any civil or criminal proceeding. Evidence of statements made in connection with any of the pleas or offers is inadmissible, except when such statements are offered in a prosecution under chapter 837.

§ 90.501. Privileges recognized only as provided

Except as otherwise provided by this chapter, any other statute, or the Constitution of the United States or of the State of Florida, no person in a legal proceeding has a privilege to:
(1) Refuse to be a witness.
(2) Refuse to disclose any matter.
(3) Refuse to produce any object or writing.
(4) Prevent another from being a witness, from disclosing any matter, or from producing any object or writing.

§ 90.5015. Journalist's privilege

(1) **Definitions**. For purposes of this section, the term:
    (a) "Professional journalist" means a person regularly engaged in collecting, photographing, recording, writing, editing, reporting,

or publishing news, for gain or livelihood, who obtained the information sought while working as a salaried employee of, or independent contractor for, a newspaper, news journal, news agency, press association, wire service, radio or television station, network, or news magazine. Book authors and others who are not professional journalists, as defined in this paragraph, are not included in the provisions of this section.

(b) "News" means information of public concern relating to local, statewide, national, or worldwide issues or events.

(2) **Privilege**. A professional journalist has a qualified privilege not to be a witness concerning, and not to disclose the information, including the identity of any source, that the professional journalist has obtained while actively gathering news. This privilege applies only to information or eyewitness observations obtained within the normal scope of employment and does not apply to physical evidence, eyewitness observations, or visual or audio recording of crimes. A party seeking to overcome this privilege must make a clear and specific showing that:

(a) The information is relevant and material to unresolved issues that have been raised in the proceeding for which the information is sought;

(b) The information cannot be obtained from alternative sources; and

(c) A compelling interest exists for requiring disclosure of the information.

(3) **Disclosure**. A court shall order disclosure pursuant to subsection (2) only of that portion of the information for which the showing under subsection (2) has been made and shall support such order with clear and specific findings made after a hearing.

(4) **Waiver**. A professional journalist does not waive the privilege by publishing or broadcasting information.

(5) **Construction**. This section must not be construed to limit any privilege or right provided to a professional journalist under law.

(6) **Authentication**. Photographs, diagrams, video recordings, audio recordings, computer records, or other business records maintained, disclosed, provided, or produced by a professional journalist, or by the employer or principal of a professional journalist, may be authenticated for admission in evidence upon a showing, by affidavit of the professional journalist, or other individual with personal knowledge, that the photograph, diagram, video recording, audio recording, computer record, or other business record is a true and

accurate copy of the original, and that the copy truly and accurately reflects the observations and facts contained therein.

(7) **Accuracy of Evidence**. If the affidavit of authenticity and accuracy, or other relevant factual circumstance, causes the court to have clear and convincing doubts as to the authenticity or accuracy of the proffered evidence, the court may decline to admit such evidence.

(8) **Severability**. If any provision of this section or its application to any particular person or circumstance is held invalid, that provision or its application is severable and does not affect the validity of other provisions or applications of this section.

§ 90.502. Lawyer-client privilege

(1) For purposes of this section:
   (a) A "lawyer" is a person authorized, or reasonably believed by the client to be authorized, to practice law in any state or nation.
   (b) A "client" is any person, public officer, corporation, association, or other organization or entity, either public or private, who consults a lawyer with the purpose of obtaining legal services or who is rendered legal services by a lawyer.
   (c) A communication between lawyer and client is "confidential" if it is not intended to be disclosed to third persons other than:
      1. Those to whom disclosure is in furtherance of the rendition of legal services to the client.
      2. Those reasonably necessary for the transmission of the communication.

(2) A client has a privilege to refuse to disclose, and to prevent any other person from disclosing, the contents of confidential communications when such other person learned of the communications because they were made in the rendition of legal services to the client.

(3) The privilege may be claimed by:
   (a) The client.
   (b) A guardian or conservator of the client.
   (c) The personal representative of a deceased client.
   (d) A successor, assignee, trustee in dissolution, or any similar representative of an organization, corporation, or association or other entity, either public or private, whether or not in existence.
   (e) The lawyer, but only on behalf of the client. The lawyer's authority to claim the privilege is presumed in the absence of contrary evidence.

(4) There is no lawyer-client privilege under this section when:

    (a) The services of the lawyer were sought or obtained to enable or aid anyone to commit or plan to commit what the client knew was a crime or fraud.

    (b) A communication is relevant to an issue between parties who claim through the same deceased client.

    (c) A communication is relevant to an issue of breach of duty by the lawyer to the client or by the client to the lawyer, arising from the lawyer-client relationship.

    (d) A communication is relevant to an issue concerning the intention or competence of a client executing an attested document to which the lawyer is an attesting witness, or concerning the execution or attestation of the document.

    (e) A communication is relevant to a matter of common interest between two or more clients, or their successors in interest, if the communication was made by any of them to a lawyer retained or consulted in common when offered in a civil action between the clients or their successors in interest.

(5) Communications made by a person who seeks or receives services from the Department of Revenue under the child support enforcement program to the attorney representing the department shall be confidential and privileged as provided for in this section. Such communications shall not be disclosed to anyone other than the agency except as provided for in this section. Such disclosures shall be protected as if there were an attorney-client relationship between the attorney for the agency and the person who seeks services from the department.

(6) A discussion or activity that is not a meeting for purposes of s. 286.011 shall not be construed to waive the attorney-client privilege established in this section. This shall not be construed to constitute an exemption to either s. 119.07 or s. 286.011.

§ 90.503. Psychotherapist-patient privilege

(1) For purposes of this section:

    (a) A "psychotherapist" is:

        1. A person authorized to practice medicine in any state or nation, or reasonably believed by the patient so to be, who is engaged in the diagnosis or treatment of a mental or

emotional condition, including alcoholism and other drug addiction;

2. A person licensed or certified as a psychologist under the laws of any state or nation, who is engaged primarily in the diagnosis or treatment of a mental or emotional condition, including alcoholism and other drug addiction;

3. A person licensed or certified as a clinical social worker, marriage and family therapist, or mental health counselor under the laws of this state, who is engaged primarily in the diagnosis or treatment of a mental or emotional condition, including alcoholism and other drug addiction;

4. Treatment personnel of facilities licensed by the state pursuant to chapter 394, chapter 395, or chapter 397, of facilities designated by the Department of Children and Family Services pursuant to chapter 394 as treatment facilities, or of facilities defined as community mental health centers pursuant to s. 394.907(1), who are engaged primarily in the diagnosis or treatment of a mental or emotional condition, including alcoholism and other drug addiction; or

5. An advanced registered nurse practitioner certified under s. 464.012, whose primary scope of practice is the diagnosis or treatment of mental or emotional conditions, including chemical abuse, and limited only to actions performed in accordance with part I of chapter 464.

(b) A "patient" is a person who consults, or is interviewed by, a psychotherapist for purposes of diagnosis or treatment of a mental or emotional condition, including alcoholism and other drug addiction.

(c) A communication between psychotherapist and patient is "confidential" if it is not intended to be disclosed to third persons other than:

1. Those persons present to further the interest of the patient in the consultation, examination, or interview.

2. Those persons necessary for the transmission of the communication.

3. Those persons who are participating in the diagnosis and treatment under the direction of the psychotherapist.

(2) A patient has a privilege to refuse to disclose, and to prevent any other person from disclosing, confidential communications or records made for the purpose of diagnosis or treatment of the patient's mental or

emotional condition, including alcoholism and other drug addiction, between the patient and the psychotherapist, or persons who are participating in the diagnosis or treatment under the direction of the psychotherapist. This privilege includes any diagnosis made, and advice given, by the psychotherapist in the course of that relationship.

(3) The privilege may be claimed by:
  (a) The patient or the patient's attorney on the patient's behalf.
  (b) A guardian or conservator of the patient.
  (c) The personal representative of a deceased patient.
  (d) The psychotherapist, but only on behalf of the patient. The authority of a psychotherapist to claim the privilege is presumed in the absence of evidence to the contrary.

(4) There is no privilege under this section:
  (a) For communications relevant to an issue in proceedings to compel hospitalization of a patient for mental illness, if the psychotherapist in the course of diagnosis or treatment has reasonable cause to believe the patient is in need of hospitalization.
  (b) For communications made in the course of a court-ordered examination of the mental or emotional condition of the patient.
  (c) For communications relevant to an issue of the mental or emotional condition of the patient in any proceeding in which the patient relies upon the condition as an element of his or her claim or defense or, after the patient's death, in any proceeding in which any party relies upon the condition as an element of the party's claim or defense.

§ 90.5035. Sexual assault counselor-victim privilege

(1) For purposes of this section:
  (a) A "rape crisis center" is any public or private agency that offers assistance to victims of sexual assault or sexual battery and their families.
  (b) A "sexual assault counselor" is any employee of a rape crisis center whose primary purpose is the rendering of advice, counseling, or assistance to victims of sexual assault or sexual battery.
  (c) A "trained volunteer" is a person who volunteers at a rape crisis center, has completed 30 hours of training in assisting victims of sexual violence and related topics provided by the rape crisis

center, is supervised by members of the staff of the rape crisis center, and is included on a list of volunteers that is maintained by the rape crisis center.

(d) A "victim" is a person who consults a sexual assault counselor or a trained volunteer for the purpose of securing advice, counseling, or assistance concerning a mental, physical, or emotional condition caused by a sexual assault or sexual battery, an alleged sexual assault or sexual battery, or an attempted sexual assault or sexual battery.

(e) A communication between a sexual assault counselor or trained volunteer and a victim is "confidential" if it is not intended to be disclosed to third persons other than:

1. Those persons present to further the interest of the victim in the consultation, examination, or interview.
2. Those persons necessary for the transmission of the communication.
3. Those persons to whom disclosure is reasonably necessary to accomplish the purposes for which the sexual assault counselor or the trained volunteer is consulted.

(2) A victim has a privilege to refuse to disclose, and to prevent any other person from disclosing, a confidential communication made by the victim to a sexual assault counselor or trained volunteer or any record made in the course of advising, counseling, or assisting the victim. Such confidential communication or record may be disclosed only with the prior written consent of the victim. This privilege includes any advice given by the sexual assault counselor or trained volunteer in the course of that relationship.

(3) The privilege may be claimed by:

(a) The victim or the victim's attorney on his or her behalf.
(b) A guardian or conservator of the victim.
(c) The personal representative of a deceased victim.
(d) The sexual assault counselor or trained volunteer, but only on behalf of the victim. The authority of a sexual assault counselor or trained volunteer to claim the privilege is presumed in the absence of evidence to the contrary.

§ 90.5036. Domestic violence advocate-victim privilege

(1) For purposes of this section:

(a) A "domestic violence center" is any public or private agency that offers assistance to victims of domestic violence, as defined in s. 741.28, and their families.

(b) A "domestic violence advocate" means any employee or volunteer who has 30 hours of training in assisting victims of domestic violence and is an employee of or volunteer for a program for victims of domestic violence whose primary purpose is the rendering of advice, counseling, or assistance to victims of domestic violence.

(c) A "victim" is a person who consults a domestic violence advocate for the purpose of securing advice, counseling, or assistance concerning a mental, physical, or emotional condition caused by an act of domestic violence, an alleged act of domestic violence, or an attempted act of domestic violence.

(d) A communication between a domestic violence advocate and a victim is "confidential" if it relates to the incident of domestic violence for which the victim is seeking assistance and if it is not intended to be disclosed to third persons other than:

    1. Those persons present to further the interest of the victim in the consultation, assessment, or interview.

    2. Those persons to whom disclosure is reasonably necessary to accomplish the purpose for which the domestic violence advocate is consulted.

(2) A victim has a privilege to refuse to disclose, and to prevent any other person from disclosing, a confidential communication made by the victim to a domestic violence advocate or any record made in the course of advising, counseling, or assisting the victim. The privilege applies to confidential communications made between the victim and the domestic violence advocate and to records of those communications only if the advocate is registered under s. 39.905 at the time the communication is made. This privilege includes any advice given by the domestic violence advocate in the course of that relationship.

(3) The privilege may be claimed by:

    (a) The victim or the victim's attorney on behalf of the victim.

    (b) A guardian or conservator of the victim.

    (c) The personal representative of a deceased victim.

    (d) The domestic violence advocate, but only on behalf of the victim. The authority of a domestic violence advocate to claim the privilege is presumed in the absence of evidence to the contrary.

§ 90.504. Husband-wife privilege

(1) A spouse has a privilege during and after the marital relationship to refuse to disclose, and to prevent another from disclosing, communications which were intended to be made in confidence between the spouses while they were husband and wife.

(2) The privilege may be claimed by either spouse or by the guardian or conservator of a spouse. The authority of a spouse, or guardian or conservator of a spouse, to claim the privilege is presumed in the absence of contrary evidence.

(3) There is no privilege under this section:
   (a) In a proceeding brought by or on behalf of one spouse against the other spouse.
   (b) In a criminal proceeding in which one spouse is charged with a crime committed at any time against the person or property of the other spouse, or the person or property of a child of either.
   (c) In a criminal proceeding in which the communication is offered in evidence by a defendant-spouse who is one of the spouses between whom the communication was made.

§ 90.505. Privilege with respect to communications to clergy

(1) For the purposes of this section:
   (a) A "member of the clergy" is a priest, rabbi, practitioner of Christian Science, or minister of any religious organization or denomination usually referred to as a church, or an individual reasonably believed so to be by the person consulting him or her.
   (b) A communication between a member of the clergy and a person is "confidential" if made privately for the purpose of seeking spiritual counsel and advice from the member of the clergy in the usual course of his or her practice or discipline and not intended for further disclosure except to other persons present in furtherance of the communication.

(2) A person has a privilege to refuse to disclose, and to prevent another from disclosing, a confidential communication by the person to a member of the clergy in his or her capacity as spiritual adviser.

(3) The privilege may be claimed by:
   (a) The person.
   (b) The guardian or conservator of a person.
   (c) The personal representative of a deceased person.

(d) The member of the clergy, on behalf of the person. The member of the clergy's authority to do so is presumed in the absence of evidence to the contrary.

§ 90.5055. Accountant-client privilege

(1) For purposes of this section:
   (a) An "accountant" is a certified public accountant or a public accountant.
   (b) A "client" is any person, public officer, corporation, association, or other organization or entity, either public or private, who consults an accountant with the purpose of obtaining accounting services.
   (c) A communication between an accountant and the accountant's client is "confidential" if it is not intended to be disclosed to third persons other than:
      1. Those to whom disclosure is in furtherance of the rendition of accounting services to the client.
      2. Those reasonably necessary for the transmission of the communication.

(2) A client has a privilege to refuse to disclose, and to prevent any other person from disclosing, the contents of confidential communications with an accountant when such other person learned of the communications because they were made in the rendition of accounting services to the client. This privilege includes other confidential information obtained by the accountant from the client for the purpose of rendering accounting advice.

(3) The privilege may be claimed by:
   (a) The client.
   (b) A guardian or conservator of the client.
   (c) The personal representative of a deceased client.
   (d) A successor, assignee, trustee in dissolution, or any similar representative of an organization, corporation, or association or other entity, either public or private, whether or not in existence.
   (e) The accountant, but only on behalf of the client. The accountant's authority to claim the privilege is presumed in the absence of contrary evidence.

(4) There is no accountant-client privilege under this section when:

(a) The services of the accountant were sought or obtained to enable or aid anyone to commit or plan to commit what the client knew or should have known was a crime or fraud.

(b) A communication is relevant to an issue of breach of duty by the accountant to the accountant's client or by the client to his or her accountant.

(c) A communication is relevant to a matter of common interest between two or more clients, if the communication was made by any of them to an accountant retained or consulted in common when offered in a civil action between the clients.

§ 90.506. Privilege with respect to trade secrets

A person has a privilege to refuse to disclose, and to prevent other persons from disclosing, a trade secret owned by that person if the allowance of the privilege will not conceal fraud or otherwise work injustice. When the court directs disclosure, it shall take the protective measures that the interests of the holder of the privilege, the interests of the parties, and the furtherance of justice require. The privilege may be claimed by the person or the person's agent or employee.

§ 90.507. Waiver of privilege by voluntary disclosure

A person who has a privilege against the disclosure of a confidential matter or communication waives the privilege if the person, or the person's predecessor while holder of the privilege, voluntarily discloses or makes the communication when he or she does not have a reasonable expectation of privacy, or consents to disclosure of, any significant part of the matter or communication. This section is not applicable when the disclosure is itself a privileged communication.

§ 90.508. Privileged matter disclosed under compulsion or without opportunity to claim privilege

Evidence of a statement or other disclosure of privileged matter is inadmissible against the holder of the privilege if the statement or disclosure was compelled erroneously by the court or made without opportunity to claim the privilege.

§ 90.509. Application of privileged communication

Nothing in this act shall abrogate a privilege for any communication which was made prior to July 1, 1979, if such communication was privileged at the time it was made.

§ 90.510. Privileged communication necessary to adverse party

In any civil case or proceeding in which a party claims a privilege as to a communication necessary to an adverse party, the court, upon motion, may dismiss the claim for relief or the affirmative defense to which the privileged testimony would relate. In making its determination, the court may engage in an in camera inquiry into the privilege.

§ 90.601. General rule of competency

Every person is competent to be a witness, except as otherwise provided by statute.

§ 90.603. Disqualification of witness

A person is disqualified to testify as a witness when the court determines that the person is:
(1) Incapable of expressing himself or herself concerning the matter in such a manner as to be understood, either directly or through interpretation by one who can understand him or her.
(2) Incapable of understanding the duty of a witness to tell the truth.

§ 90.604. Lack of personal knowledge

Except as otherwise provided in s. 90.702, a witness may not testify to a matter unless evidence is introduced which is sufficient to support a finding that the witness has personal knowledge of the matter. Evidence to prove personal knowledge may be given by the witness's own testimony.

§ 90.605. Oath or affirmation of witness

(1) Before testifying, each witness shall declare that he or she will testify truthfully, by taking an oath or affirmation in substantially the following form: "Do you swear or affirm that the evidence you are about to give will be the truth, the whole truth, and nothing but the truth?" The witness's answer shall be noted in the record.

(2) In the court's discretion, a child may testify without taking the oath if the court determines the child understands the duty to tell the truth or the duty not to lie.

§ 90.606. Interpreters and translators

(1)

    (a) When a judge determines that a witness cannot hear or understand the English language, or cannot express himself or herself in English sufficiently to be understood, an interpreter who is duly qualified to interpret for the witness shall be sworn to do so.

    (b) This section is not limited to persons who speak a language other than English, but applies also to the language and descriptions of any person, such as a child or a person who is mentally or developmentally disabled, who cannot be reasonably understood, or who cannot understand questioning, without the aid of an interpreter.

(2) A person who serves in the role of interpreter or translator in any action or proceeding is subject to all the provisions of this chapter relating to witnesses.

(3) An interpreter shall take an oath that he or she will make a true interpretation of the questions asked and the answers given and that the interpreter will make a true translation into English of any writing which he or she is required by his or her duties to decipher or translate.

§ 90.6063. Interpreter services for deaf persons

(1) The Legislature finds that it is an important concern that the rights of deaf citizens be protected. It is the intent of the Legislature to ensure that appropriate and effective interpreter services be made available to Florida's deaf citizens.

(2) In all judicial proceedings and in sessions of a grand jury wherein a deaf person is a complainant, defendant, witness, or otherwise a party, or wherein a deaf person is a juror or grand juror, the court or presiding officer shall appoint a qualified interpreter to interpret the proceedings or deliberations to the deaf person and to interpret the deaf person's testimony, statements, or deliberations to the court, jury, or grand jury. A qualified interpreter shall be appointed, or other auxiliary aid provided as appropriate, for the duration of the trial or other proceeding in which a deaf juror or grand juror is seated.

(3)

(a) "Deaf person" means any person whose hearing is so seriously impaired as to prohibit the person from understanding oral communications when spoken in a normal, conversational tone.

(b) For the purposes of this section, the term "qualified interpreter" means an interpreter certified by the National Registry of Interpreters for the Deaf or the Florida Registry of Interpreters for the Deaf or an interpreter whose qualifications are otherwise determined by the appointing authority.

(4) Every deaf person whose appearance before a proceeding entitles him or her to an interpreter shall notify the appointing authority of his or her disability not less than 5 days prior to any appearance and shall request at such time the services of an interpreter. Whenever a deaf person receives notification of the time of an appearance before a proceeding less than 5 days prior to the proceeding, the deaf person shall provide his or her notification and request as soon thereafter as practicable. In any case, nothing in this subsection shall operate to relieve an appointing authority's duty to provide an interpreter for a deaf person so entitled, and failure to strictly comply with the notice requirement will not be deemed a waiver of the right to an interpreter. An appointing authority may require a person requesting the appointment of an interpreter to furnish reasonable proof of the person's disability when the appointing authority has reason to believe that the person is not so disabled.

(5) The appointing authority may channel requests for qualified interpreters through:

(a) The Florida Registry of Interpreters for the Deaf;

(b) The Division of Vocational Rehabilitation of the Department of Education; or

(c) Any other resource wherein the appointing authority knows that qualified interpreters can be found.

(6) No qualified interpreter shall be appointed unless the appointing authority and the deaf person make a preliminary determination that the interpreter is able to communicate readily with the deaf person and is able to repeat and translate statements to and from the deaf person accurately.

(7) Before a qualified interpreter may participate in any proceedings subsequent to an appointment under the provisions of this act, such interpreter shall make an oath or affirmation that he or she will make a true interpretation in an understandable manner to the deaf person for whom the interpreter is appointed and that he or she will repeat the

statements of the deaf person in the English language to the best of his or her skill and judgment. Whenever a deaf person communicates through an interpreter to any person under such circumstances that the communication would be privileged, and the recipient of the communication could not be compelled to testify as to the communication, this privilege shall apply to the interpreter.

(8) An interpreter appointed by the court in a criminal matter or in a civil matter shall be entitled to a reasonable fee for such service, in addition to actual expenses for travel, to be paid out of general county funds.

§ 90.607. Competency of certain persons as witnesses

(1)

    (a) Except as provided in paragraph (b), the judge presiding at the trial of an action is not competent to testify as a witness in that trial. An objection is not necessary to preserve the point.

    (b) By agreement of the parties, the trial judge may give evidence on a purely formal matter to facilitate the trial of the action.

(2)

    (a) A member of the jury is not competent to testify as a witness in a trial when he or she is sitting as a juror. If the juror is called to testify, the opposing party shall be given an opportunity to object out of the presence of the jury.

    (b) Upon an inquiry into the validity of a verdict or indictment, a juror is not competent to testify as to any matter which essentially inheres in the verdict or indictment.

§ 90.608. Who may impeach

Any party, including the party calling the witness, may attack the credibility of a witness by:

(1) Introducing statements of the witness which are inconsistent with the witness's present testimony.

(2) Showing that the witness is biased.

(3) Attacking the character of the witness in accordance with the provisions of s. 90.609 or s. 90.610.

(4) Showing a defect of capacity, ability, or opportunity in the witness to observe, remember, or recount the matters about which the witness testified.

(5) Proof by other witnesses that material facts are not as testified to by the witness being impeached.

§ 90.609. Character of witness as impeachment

A party may attack or support the credibility of a witness, including an accused, by evidence in the form of reputation, except that:

(1) The evidence may refer only to character relating to truthfulness.

(2) Evidence of a truthful character is admissible only after the character of the witness for truthfulness has been attacked by reputation evidence.

§ 90.610. Conviction of certain crimes as impeachment

(1) A party may attack the credibility of any witness, including an accused, by evidence that the witness has been convicted of a crime if the crime was punishable by death or imprisonment in excess of 1 year under the law under which the witness was convicted, or if the crime involved dishonesty or a false statement regardless of the punishment, with the following exceptions:

(a) Evidence of any such conviction is inadmissible in a civil trial if it is so remote in time as to have no bearing on the present character of the witness.

(b) Evidence of juvenile adjudications are inadmissible under this subsection.

(2) The pendency of an appeal or the granting of a pardon relating to such crime does not render evidence of the conviction from which the appeal was taken or for which the pardon was granted inadmissible. Evidence of the pendency of the appeal is admissible.

(3) Nothing in this section affects the admissibility of evidence under s. 90.404 or s. 90.608.

§ 90.611. Religious beliefs or opinions

Evidence of the beliefs or opinions of a witness on matters of religion is inadmissible to show that the witness's credibility is impaired or enhanced thereby.

§ 90.612. Mode and order of interrogation and presentation

(1) The judge shall exercise reasonable control over the mode and order of the interrogation of witnesses and the presentation of evidence, so as to:

(a) Facilitate, through effective interrogation and presentation, the discovery of the truth.

(b) Avoid needless consumption of time.

(c) Protect witnesses from harassment or undue embarrassment.

(2) Cross-examination of a witness is limited to the subject matter of the direct examination and matters affecting the credibility of the witness. The court may, in its discretion, permit inquiry into additional matters.

(3) Leading questions should not be used on the direct examination of a witness except as may be necessary to develop the witness's testimony. Ordinarily, leading questions should be permitted on cross-examination. When a party calls a hostile witness, an adverse party, or a witness identified with an adverse party, interrogation may be by leading questions.

The judge shall take special care to protect a witness under age 14 from questions that are in a form that cannot reasonably be understood by a person of the age and understanding of the witness, and shall take special care to restrict the unnecessary repetition of questions.

§ 90.613. Refreshing the memory of a witness

When a witness uses a writing or other item to refresh memory while testifying, an adverse party is entitled to have such writing or other item produced at the hearing, to inspect it, to cross-examine the witness thereon, and to introduce it, or, in the case of a writing, to introduce those portions which relate to the testimony of the witness, in evidence. If it is claimed that the writing contains matters not related to the subject matter of the testimony, the judge shall examine the writing in camera, excise any portions not so related, and order delivery of the remainder to the party entitled thereto. Any portion withheld over objection shall be preserved and made available to the appellate court in the event of an appeal. If a writing or other item is not produced or delivered pursuant to order under this section, the testimony of the witness concerning those matters shall be stricken.

§ 90.614. Prior statements of witnesses

(1) When a witness is examined concerning the witness's prior written statement or concerning an oral statement that has been reduced to writing, the court, on motion of the adverse party, shall order the statement to be shown to the witness or its contents disclosed to him or her.

(2) Extrinsic evidence of a prior inconsistent statement by a witness is inadmissible unless the witness is first afforded an opportunity to explain or deny the prior statement and the opposing party is afforded an opportunity to interrogate the witness on it, or the interests of justice otherwise require. If a witness denies making or does not distinctly admit making the prior inconsistent statement, extrinsic evidence of such statement is admissible. This subsection is not applicable to admissions of a party-opponent as defined in s. 90.803(18).

§ 90.615. Calling witnesses by the court

(1) The court may call witnesses whom all parties may cross-examine.
(2) When required by the interests of justice, the court may interrogate witnesses, whether called by the court or by a party.

§ 90.616. Exclusion of witnesses

(1) At the request of a party the court shall order, or upon its own motion the court may order, witnesses excluded from a proceeding so that they cannot hear the testimony of other witnesses except as provided in subsection (2).
(2) A witness may not be excluded if the witness is:
    (a) A party who is a natural person.
    (b) In a civil case, an officer or employee of a party that is not a natural person. The party's attorney shall designate the officer or employee who shall be the party's representative.
    (c) A person whose presence is shown by the party's attorney to be essential to the presentation of the party's cause.
    (d) In a criminal case, the victim of the crime, the victim's next of kin, the parent or guardian of a minor child victim, or a lawful representative of such person, unless, upon motion, the court determines such person's presence to be prejudicial.

§ 90.701. Opinion testimony of lay witnesses

If a witness is not testifying as an expert, the witness's testimony about what he or she perceived may be in the form of inference and opinion when:
(1) The witness cannot readily, and with equal accuracy and adequacy, communicate what he or she has perceived to the trier of fact without

testifying in terms of inferences or opinions and the witness's use of inferences or opinions will not mislead the trier of fact to the prejudice of the objecting party; and

(2) The opinions and inferences do not require a special knowledge, skill, experience, or training.

§ 90.702. Testimony by experts

If scientific, technical, or other specialized knowledge will assist the trier of fact in understanding the evidence or in determining a fact in issue, a witness qualified as an expert by knowledge, skill, experience, training, or education may testify about it in the form of an opinion or otherwise, if:

(1) The testimony is based upon sufficient facts or data;

(2) The testimony is the product of reliable principles and methods; and

(3) The witness has applied the principles and methods reliably to the facts of the case.

§ 90.703. Opinion on ultimate issue

Testimony in the form of an opinion or inference otherwise admissible is not objectionable because it includes an ultimate issue to be decided by the trier of fact.

§ 90.704. Basis of opinion testimony by experts

The facts or data upon which an expert bases an opinion or inference may be those perceived by, or made known to, the expert at or before the trial. If the facts or data are of a type reasonably relied upon by experts in the subject to support the opinion expressed, the facts or data need not be admissible in evidence. Facts or data that are otherwise inadmissible may not be disclosed to the jury by the proponent of the opinion or inference unless the court determines that their probative value in assisting the jury to evaluate the expert's opinion substantially outweighs their prejudicial effect.

§ 90.705. Disclosure of facts or data underlying expert opinion

(1) Unless otherwise required by the court, an expert may testify in terms of opinion or inferences and give reasons without prior disclosure of the underlying facts or data. On cross-examination the expert shall be required to specify the facts or data.

(2) Prior to the witness giving the opinion, a party against whom the opinion or inference is offered may conduct a voir dire examination of the witness directed to the underlying facts or data for the witness's opinion. If the party establishes prima facie evidence that the expert does not have a sufficient basis for the opinion, the opinions and inferences of the expert are inadmissible unless the party offering the testimony establishes the underlying facts or data.

§ 90.706. Authoritativeness of literature for use in cross-examination

Statements of facts or opinions on a subject of science, art, or specialized knowledge contained in a published treatise, periodical, book, dissertation, pamphlet, or other writing may be used in cross-examination of an expert witness if the expert witness recognizes the author or the treatise, periodical, book, dissertation, pamphlet, or other writing to be authoritative, or, notwithstanding nonrecognition by the expert witness, if the trial court finds the author or the treatise, periodical, book, dissertation, pamphlet, or other writing to be authoritative and relevant to the subject matter.

§ 90.801. Hearsay; definitions; exceptions

(1) The following definitions apply under this chapter:
    (a) A "statement" is:
        1. An oral or written assertion; or
        2. Nonverbal conduct of a person if it is intended by the person as an assertion.
    (b) A "declarant" is a person who makes a statement.
    (c) "Hearsay" is a statement, other than one made by the declarant while testifying at the trial or hearing, offered in evidence to prove the truth of the matter asserted.
(2) A statement is not hearsay if the declarant testifies at the trial or hearing and is subject to cross-examination concerning the statement and the statement is:
    (a) Inconsistent with the declarant's testimony and was given under oath subject to the penalty of perjury at a trial, hearing, or other proceeding or in a deposition;
    (b) Consistent with the declarant's testimony and is offered to rebut an express or implied charge against the declarant of improper influence, motive, or recent fabrication; or

(c) One of identification of a person made after perceiving the person.

§ 90.802. Hearsay rule

Except as provided by statute, hearsay evidence is inadmissible.

§ 90.803. Hearsay exceptions; availability of declarant immaterial

The provision of s. 90.802 to the contrary notwithstanding, the following are not inadmissible as evidence, even though the declarant is available as a witness:

(1) **Spontaneous Statement**. A spontaneous statement describing or explaining an event or condition made while the declarant was perceiving the event or condition, or immediately thereafter, except when such statement is made under circumstances that indicate its lack of trustworthiness.

(2) **Excited Utterance**. A statement or excited utterance relating to a startling event or condition made while the declarant was under the stress of excitement caused by the event or condition.

(3) **Then-Existing Mental, Emotional, Or Physical Condition**.
   (a) A statement of the declarant's then-existing state of mind, emotion, or physical sensation, including a statement of intent, plan, motive, design, mental feeling, pain, or bodily health, when such evidence is offered to:
      1. Prove the declarant's state of mind, emotion, or physical sensation at that time or at any other time when such state is an issue in the action.
      2. Prove or explain acts of subsequent conduct of the declarant.
   (b) However, this subsection does not make admissible:
      1. An after-the-fact statement of memory or belief to prove the fact remembered or believed, unless such statement relates to the execution, revocation, identification, or terms of the declarant's will.
      2. A statement made under circumstances that indicate its lack of trustworthiness.

(4) **Statements for Purposes of Medical Diagnosis or Treatment**. Statements made for purposes of medical diagnosis or treatment by a person seeking the diagnosis or treatment, or made by an individual who has knowledge of the facts and is legally responsible for the person who is unable to communicate the facts, which statements

describe medical history, past or present symptoms, pain, or sensations, or the inceptions or general character of the cause or external source thereof, insofar as reasonably pertinent to diagnosis or treatment.

(5) **Recorded Recollection**. A memorandum or record concerning a matter about which a witness once had knowledge, but now has insufficient recollection to enable the witness to testify fully and accurately, shown to have been made by the witness when the matter was fresh in the witness's memory and to reflect that knowledge correctly. A party may read into evidence a memorandum or record when it is admitted, but no such memorandum or record is admissible as an exhibit unless offered by an adverse party.

(6) **Records of Regularly Conducted Business Activity**.

    (a) A memorandum, report, record, or data compilation, in any form, of acts, events, conditions, opinion, or diagnosis, made at or near the time by, or from information transmitted by, a person with knowledge, if kept in the course of a regularly conducted business activity and if it was the regular practice of that business activity to make such memorandum, report, record, or data compilation, all as shown by the testimony of the custodian or other qualified witness, or as shown by a certification or declaration that complies with paragraph (c) and s. 90.902(11), unless the sources of information or other circumstances show lack of trustworthiness. The term "business" as used in this paragraph includes a business, institution, association, profession, occupation, and calling of every kind, whether or not conducted for profit.

    (b) Evidence in the form of an opinion or diagnosis is inadmissible under paragraph (a) unless such opinion or diagnosis would be admissible under ss. 90.701-90.705 if the person whose opinion is recorded were to testify to the opinion directly.

    (c) A party intending to offer evidence under paragraph (a) by means of a certification or declaration shall serve reasonable written notice of that intention upon every other party and shall make the evidence available for inspection sufficiently in advance of its offer in evidence to provide to any other party a fair opportunity to challenge the admissibility of the evidence. If the evidence is maintained in a foreign country, the party intending to offer the evidence must provide written notice of that intention at the arraignment or as soon after the arraignment as is practicable or, in a civil case, 60 days before the trial. A motion opposing the admissibility of such evidence must be made by the opposing party and determined by the court before trial. A party's failure to file such a motion before trial constitutes a waiver of objection to the evidence, but the court for good cause shown may grant relief from the waiver.

(7) **Absence of Entry in Records of Regularly Conducted Activity**. Evidence that a matter is not included in the memoranda, reports, records, or data compilations, in any form, of a regularly conducted activity to prove the nonoccurrence or nonexistence of the matter, if the matter was of a kind of which a memorandum, report, record, or data compilation was regularly made and preserved, unless the sources of information or other circumstances show lack of trustworthiness.

(8) **Public Records and Reports**. Records, reports, statements reduced to writing, or data compilations, in any form, of public offices or agencies, setting forth the activities of the office or agency, or matters observed pursuant to duty imposed by law as to matters which there was a duty to report, excluding in criminal cases matters observed by a police officer or other law enforcement personnel, unless the sources of information or other circumstances show their lack of trustworthiness. The criminal case exclusion shall not apply to an affidavit otherwise admissible under s. 316.1934 or s. 327.354.

(9) **Records Of Vital Statistics**. Records or data compilations, in any form, of births, fetal deaths, deaths, or marriages, if a report was made to a public office pursuant to requirements of law. However, nothing in this section shall be construed to make admissible any other marriage of any party to any cause of action except for the purpose of impeachment as set forth in s. 90.610.

(10) **Absence of Public Record or Entry**. Evidence, in the form of a certification in accord with s. 90.902, or in the form of testimony, that diligent search failed to disclose a record, report, statement, or data compilation or entry, when offered to prove the absence of the record, report, statement, or data compilation or the nonoccurrence or nonexistence of a matter of which a record, report, statement, or data compilation would regularly have been made and preserved by a public office and agency.

(11) **Records of Religious Organizations**. Statements of births, marriages, divorces, deaths, parentage, ancestry, relationship by blood or marriage, or other similar facts of personal or family history contained in a regularly kept record of a religious organization.

(12) **Marriage, Baptismal, and Similar Certificates**. Statements of facts contained in a certificate that the maker performed a marriage or other ceremony or administered a sacrament, when such statement was certified by a member of the clergy, public official, or other person authorized by the rules or practices of a religious organization or by law to perform the act certified, and when such certificate purports to have been issued at the time of the act or within a reasonable time thereafter.

(13) **Family Records**. Statements of fact concerning personal or family history in family Bibles, charts, engravings in rings, inscriptions on family portraits, engravings on urns, crypts, or tombstones, or the like.

(14) **Records of Documents Affecting an Interest in Property**. The record of a document purporting to establish or affect an interest in property, as proof of the contents of the original recorded or filed document and its execution and delivery by each person by whom it purports to have been executed, if the record is a record of a public office and an applicable statute authorized the recording or filing of the document in the office.

(15) **Statements in Documents Affecting an Interest in Property**. A statement contained in a document purporting to establish or affect an interest in property, if the matter stated was relevant to the purpose of the document, unless dealings with the property since the document was made have been inconsistent with the truth of the statement or the purport of the document.

(16) **Statements in Ancient Documents**. Statements in a document in existence 20 years or more, the authenticity of which is established.

(17) **Market Reports, Commercial Publications**. Market quotations, tabulations, lists, directories, or other published compilations, generally used and relied upon by the public or by persons in particular occupations if, in the opinion of the court, the sources of information and method of preparation were such as to justify their admission.

(18) **Admissions**. A statement that is offered against a party and is:
  (a) The party's own statement in either an individual or a representative capacity;
  (b) A statement of which the party has manifested an adoption or belief in its truth;
  (c) A statement by a person specifically authorized by the party to make a statement concerning the subject;

(d) A statement by the party's agent or servant concerning a matter within the scope of the agency or employment thereof, made during the existence of the relationship; or

(e) A statement by a person who was a coconspirator of the party during the course, and in furtherance, of the conspiracy. Upon request of counsel, the court shall instruct the jury that the conspiracy itself and each member's participation in it must be established by independent evidence, either before the introduction of any evidence or before evidence is admitted under this paragraph.

(19) **Reputation Concerning Personal or Family History**. Evidence of reputation:

(a) Among members of a person's family by blood, adoption, or marriage;

(b) Among a person's associates; or

(c) In the community,

concerning a person's birth, adoption, marriage, divorce, death, relationship by blood, adoption, or marriage, ancestry, or other similar fact of personal or family history.

(20) **Reputation Concerning Boundaries or General History**. Evidence of reputation:

(a) In a community, arising before the controversy about the boundaries of, or customs affecting lands in, the community.

(b) About events of general history which are important to the community, state, or nation where located.

(21) **Reputation as to Character**. Evidence of reputation of a person's character among associates or in the community.

(22) **Former Testimony**. Former testimony given by the declarant which testimony was given as a witness at another hearing of the same or a different proceeding, or in a deposition taken in compliance with law in the course of the same or another proceeding, if the party against whom the testimony is now offered, or, in a civil action or proceeding, a predecessor in interest, or a person with a similar interest, had an opportunity and similar motive to develop the testimony by direct, cross, or redirect examination; provided, however, the court finds that the testimony is not inadmissible pursuant to s. 90.402 or s. 90.403.

(23) **Hearsay Exception; Statement of Child Victim**.

(a) Unless the source of information or the method or circumstances by which the statement is reported indicates a lack of trustworthiness, an out-of-court statement made by a child victim with a physical, mental, emotional, or developmental age of 16 or less describing any act of child abuse or neglect, any act of sexual abuse against a child, the offense of child abuse, the offense of aggravated child abuse, or any offense involving an unlawful sexual act, contact, intrusion, or penetration performed in the presence of, with, by, or on the declarant child, not otherwise admissible, is admissible in evidence in any civil or criminal proceeding if:

1. The court finds in a hearing conducted outside the presence of the jury that the time, content, and circumstances of the statement provide sufficient safeguards of reliability. In making its determination, the court may consider the mental and physical age and maturity of the child, the nature and duration of the abuse or offense, the relationship of the child to the offender, the reliability of the assertion, the reliability of the child victim, and any other factor deemed appropriate; and

2. The child either:
   a. Testifies; or
   b. Is unavailable as a witness, provided that there is other corroborative evidence of the abuse or offense. Unavailability shall include a finding by the court that the child's participation in the trial or proceeding would result in a substantial likelihood of severe emotional or mental harm, in addition to findings pursuant to s. 90.804(1).

(b) In a criminal action, the defendant shall be notified no later than 10 days before trial that a statement which qualifies as a hearsay exception pursuant to this subsection will be offered as evidence at trial. The notice shall include a written statement of the content of the child's statement, the time at which the statement was made, the circumstances surrounding the statement which indicate its reliability, and such other particulars as necessary to provide full disclosure of the statement.

(c) The court shall make specific findings of fact, on the record, as to the basis for its ruling under this subsection.

(24) **Hearsay Exception; Statement of Elderly Person or Disabled Adult.**

(a) Unless the source of information or the method or circumstances by which the statement is reported indicates a lack of trustworthiness, an out-of-court statement made by an elderly person or disabled adult, as defined in s. 825.101, describing any act of abuse or neglect, any act of exploitation, the offense of battery or aggravated battery or assault or aggravated assault or sexual battery, or any other violent act on the declarant elderly person or disabled adult, not otherwise admissible, is admissible in evidence in any civil or criminal proceeding if:

1. The court finds in a hearing conducted outside the presence of the jury that the time, content, and circumstances of the statement provide sufficient safeguards of reliability. In making its determination, the court may consider the mental and physical age and maturity of the elderly person or disabled adult, the nature and duration of the abuse or offense, the relationship of the victim to the offender, the reliability of the assertion, the reliability of the elderly person or disabled adult, and any other factor deemed appropriate; and

2. The elderly person or disabled adult is unavailable as a witness, provided that there is corroborative evidence of the abuse or offense. Unavailability shall include a finding by the court that the elderly person's or disabled adult's participation in the trial or proceeding would result in a substantial likelihood of severe emotional, mental, or physical harm, in addition to findings pursuant to s. 90.804(1).

(b) In a criminal action, the defendant shall be notified no later than 10 days before the trial that a statement which qualifies as a hearsay exception pursuant to this subsection will be offered as evidence at trial. The notice shall include a written statement of the content of the elderly person's or disabled adult's statement, the time at which the statement was made, the circumstances surrounding the statement which indicate its reliability, and such other particulars as necessary to provide full disclosure of the statement.

(c) The court shall make specific findings of fact, on the record, as to the basis for its ruling under this subsection.

§ 90.804. Hearsay exceptions; declarant unavailable

(1) **Definition of Unavailability**. "Unavailability as a witness" means that the declarant:

    (a) Is exempted by a ruling of a court on the ground of privilege from testifying concerning the subject matter of the declarant's statement;

    (b) Persists in refusing to testify concerning the subject matter of the declarant's statement despite an order of the court to do so;

    (c) Has suffered a lack of memory of the subject matter of his or her statement so as to destroy the declarant's effectiveness as a witness during the trial;

    (d) Is unable to be present or to testify at the hearing because of death or because of then-existing physical or mental illness or infirmity; or

    (e) Is absent from the hearing, and the proponent of a statement has been unable to procure the declarant's attendance or testimony by process or other reasonable means.

However, a declarant is not unavailable as a witness if such exemption, refusal, claim of lack of memory, inability to be present, or absence is due to the procurement or wrongdoing of the party who is the proponent of his or her statement in preventing the witness from attending or testifying.

(2) **Hearsay Exceptions**. The following are not excluded under s. 90.802, provided that the declarant is unavailable as a witness:

    (a) Former testimony. Testimony given as a witness at another hearing of the same or a different proceeding, or in a deposition taken in compliance with law in the course of the same or another proceeding, if the party against whom the testimony is now offered, or, in a civil action or proceeding, a predecessor in interest, had an opportunity and similar motive to develop the testimony by direct, cross, or redirect examination.

    (b) Statement under belief of impending death. In a civil or criminal trial, a statement made by a declarant while reasonably believing that his or her death was imminent, concerning the physical cause or instrumentalities of what the declarant believed to be impending death or the circumstances surrounding impending death.

    (c) Statement against interest. A statement which, at the time of its making, was so far contrary to the declarant's pecuniary or proprietary interest or tended to subject the declarant to liability or to render invalid a claim by the declarant against another, so that a person in the declarant's position would not have made the statement unless he or she believed it to be true. A statement tending to expose the declarant to criminal liability and offered to exculpate the accused is inadmissible, unless corroborating circumstances show the trustworthiness of the statement.

(d) Statement of personal or family history. A statement concerning the declarant's own birth, adoption, marriage, divorce, parentage, ancestry, or other similar fact of personal or family history, including relationship by blood, adoption, or marriage, even though the declarant had no means of acquiring personal knowledge of the matter stated.

(e) Statement by deceased or ill declarant similar to one previously admitted. In an action or proceeding brought against the personal representative, heir at law, assignee, legatee, devisee, or survivor of a deceased person, or against a trustee of a trust created by a deceased person, or against the assignee, committee, or guardian of a mentally incompetent person, when a declarant is unavailable as provided in paragraph (1)(d), a written or oral statement made regarding the same subject matter as another statement made by the declarant that has previously been offered by an adverse party and admitted in evidence.

(f) Statement offered against a party that wrongfully caused the declarant's unavailability. A statement offered against a party that wrongfully caused, or acquiesced in wrongfully causing, the declarant's unavailability as a witness, and did so intending that result.

§ 90.805. Hearsay within hearsay

Hearsay within hearsay is not excluded under s. 90.802, provided each part of the combined statements conforms with an exception to the hearsay rule as provided in s. 90.803 or s. 90.804.

§ 90.806. Attacking and supporting credibility of declarant

(1) When a hearsay statement has been admitted in evidence, credibility of the declarant may be attacked and, if attacked, may be supported by any evidence that would be admissible for those purposes if the declarant had testified as a witness. Evidence of a statement or conduct

by the declarant at any time inconsistent with the declarant's hearsay statement is admissible, regardless of whether or not the declarant has been afforded an opportunity to deny or explain it.

(2) If the party against whom a hearsay statement has been admitted calls the declarant as a witness, the party is entitled to examine the declarant on the statement as if under cross-examination.

§ 90.901. Requirement of authentication or identification

Authentication or identification of evidence is required as a condition precedent to its admissibility. The requirements of this section are satisfied by evidence sufficient to support a finding that the matter in question is what its proponent claims.

§ 90.902. Self-authentication

Extrinsic evidence of authenticity as a condition precedent to admissibility is not required for:

(1) A document bearing:
   (a) A seal purporting to be that of the United States or any state, district, commonwealth, territory, or insular possession thereof; the Panama Canal Zone; the Trust Territory of the Pacific Islands; or a court, political subdivision, department, officer, or agency of any of them; and
   (b) A signature by the custodian of the document attesting to the authenticity of the seal.
(2) A document not bearing a seal but purporting to bear a signature of an officer or employee of any entity listed in subsection (1), affixed in the officer's or employee's official capacity.
(3) An official foreign document, record, or entry that is:
   (a) Executed or attested to by a person in the person's official capacity authorized by the laws of a foreign country to make the execution or attestation; and
   (b) Accompanied by a final certification, as provided herein, of the genuineness of the signature and official position of:
      1. The executing person; or
      2. Any foreign official whose certificate of genuineness of signature and official position relates to the execution or attestation or is in a chain of certificates of genuineness of signature and official position relating to the execution or attestation.

The final certification may be made by a secretary of an embassy or legation, consul general, consul, vice consul, or consular agent of the United States or a diplomatic or consular official of the foreign country assigned or accredited to the United States. When the parties receive reasonable opportunity to investigate the authenticity and accuracy of official foreign documents, the court may order that they be treated as presumptively authentic without final certification or permit them in evidence by an attested summary with or without final certification.

(4) A copy of an official public record, report, or entry, or of a document authorized by law to be recorded or filed and actually recorded or filed in a public office, including data compilations in any form, certified as correct by the custodian or other person authorized to make the certification by certificate complying with subsection (1), subsection (2), or subsection (3) or complying with any act of the Legislature or rule adopted by the Supreme Court.

(5) Books, pamphlets, or other publications purporting to be issued by a governmental authority.

(6) Printed materials purporting to be newspapers or periodicals.

(7) Inscriptions, signs, tags, or labels purporting to have been affixed in the course of business and indicating ownership, control, or origin.

(8) Commercial papers and signatures thereon and documents relating to them, to the extent provided in the Uniform Commercial Code.

(9) Any signature, document, or other matter declared by the Legislature to be presumptively or prima facie genuine or authentic.

(10) Any document properly certified under the law of the jurisdiction where the certification is made.

(11) An original or a duplicate of evidence that would be admissible under s. 90.803(6), which is maintained in a foreign country or domestic location and is accompanied by a certification or declaration from the custodian of the records or another qualified person certifying or declaring that the record:

(a) Was made at or near the time of the occurrence of the matters set forth by, or from information transmitted by, a person having knowledge of those matters;

(b) Was kept in the course of the regularly conducted activity; and

(c) Was made as a regular practice in the course of the regularly conducted activity, provided that falsely making such a certification or declaration would subject the maker to criminal penalty under the laws of the foreign or domestic location in which the certification or declaration was signed.

§ 90.903. Testimony of subscribing witness unnecessary

The testimony of a subscribing witness is not necessary to authenticate a writing unless the statute requiring attestation requires it.

§ 90.91. Photographs of property wrongfully taken; use in prosecution, procedure; return of property to owner

In any prosecution for a crime involving the wrongful taking of property, a photograph of the property alleged to have been wrongfully taken may be deemed competent evidence of such property and may be admissible in the prosecution to the same extent as if such property were introduced as evidence. Such photograph shall bear a written description of the property alleged to have been wrongfully taken, the name of the owner of the property, the location where the alleged wrongful taking occurred, the name of the investigating law enforcement officer, the date the photograph was taken, and the name of the photographer. Such writing shall be made under oath by the investigating law enforcement officer, and the photograph shall be identified by the signature of the photographer. Upon the filing of such photograph and writing with the law enforcement authority or court holding such property as evidence, the property may be returned to the owner from whom the property was taken.

§ 90.951. Definitions

For purposes of this chapter:
(1) "Writings" and "recordings" include letters, words, or numbers, or their equivalent, set down by handwriting, typewriting, printing, photostating, photography, magnetic impulse, mechanical or electronic recording, or other form of data compilation, upon paper, wood, stone, recording tape, or other materials.
(2) "Photographs" include still photographs, X-ray films, videotapes, and motion pictures.
(3) An "original" of a writing or recording means the writing or recording itself, or any counterpart intended to have the same effect by a person executing or issuing it. An "original" of a photograph includes the negative or any print made from it. If data are stored in a computer or

similar device, any printout or other output readable by sight and shown to reflect the data accurately is an "original."

(4) "Duplicate" includes:

    (a) A counterpart produced by the same impression as the original, from the same matrix; by means of photography, including enlargements and miniatures; by mechanical or electronic rerecording; by chemical reproduction; or by other equivalent technique that accurately reproduces the original; or

    (b) An executed carbon copy not intended by the parties to be an original.

§ 90.952. Requirement of originals

Except as otherwise provided by statute, an original writing, recording, or photograph is required in order to prove the contents of the writing, recording, or photograph.

§ 90.953. Admissibility of duplicates

A duplicate is admissible to the same extent as an original, unless:

(1) The document or writing is a negotiable instrument as defined in s. 673.1041, a security as defined in s. 678.1021, or any other writing that evidences a right to the payment of money, is not itself a security agreement or lease, and is of a type that is transferred by delivery in the ordinary course of business with any necessary endorsement or assignment.

(2) A genuine question is raised about the authenticity of the original or any other document or writing.

(3) It is unfair, under the circumstance, to admit the duplicate in lieu of the original.

§ 90.954. Admissibility of other evidence of contents

The original of a writing, recording, or photograph is not required, except as provided in s. 90.953, and other evidence of its contents is admissible when:

(1) All originals are lost or destroyed, unless the proponent lost or destroyed them in bad faith.

(2) An original cannot be obtained in this state by any judicial process or procedure.

(3) An original was under the control of the party against whom offered at a time when that party was put on notice by the pleadings or by written notice from the adverse party that the contents of such original would be subject to proof at the hearing, and such original is not produced at the hearing.

(4) The writing, recording, or photograph is not related to a controlling issue.

§ 90.955. Public records

(1) The contents of an official record or of a document authorized to be recorded or filed, and actually recorded or filed, with a governmental agency, either federal, state, county, or municipal, in a place where official records or documents are ordinarily filed, including data compilations in any form, may be proved by a copy authenticated as provided in s. 90.902, if otherwise admissible.

(2) If a party cannot obtain, by the exercise of reasonable diligence, a copy that complies with subsection (1), other evidence of the contents is admissible.

§ 90.956. Summaries

When it is not convenient to examine in court the contents of voluminous writings, recordings, or photographs, a party may present them in the form of a chart, summary, or calculation by calling a qualified witness. The party intending to use such a summary must give timely written notice of his or her intention to use the summary, proof of which shall be filed with the court, and shall make the summary and the originals or duplicates of the data from which the summary is compiled available for examination or copying, or both, by other parties at a reasonable time and place. A judge may order that they be produced in court.

§ 90.957. Testimony or written admissions of a party

A party may prove the contents of writings, recordings, or photographs by the testimony or deposition of the party against whom they are offered or by that party's written admission, without accounting for the nonproduction of the original.

§ 90.958. Functions of court and jury

(1) Except as provided in subsection (2), when the admissibility under this chapter of other evidence of the contents of writings, recordings, or photographs depends upon the existence of a preliminary fact, the question as to whether the preliminary fact exists is for the court to determine.

(2) The trier of fact shall determine whether:
   (a) The asserted writing ever existed.
   (b) Another writing, recording, or photograph produced at the trial is the original.
   (c) Other evidence of the contents correctly reflects the contents.